Daily Rituals

Positive Affirmations to Attract Love, Happiness and Peace.

By Phoebe Garnsworthy

This book was written by Phoebe Garnsworthy,

visionary and metaphysical writer.

Other Books by Phoebe Garnsworthy:

Lost Nowhere

The Spirit Guides

Artwork by Troiscentdanses

ISBN: 978-0-9954119-8-2

www.PhoebeGarnsworthy.com

DEDICATION

This book is dedicated to Your Higher Self.

To the beautiful Spirit inside of You that deserves to be

honored, loved and respected.

My gratitude to You is eternal.

Contents

Personal Notes

Introduction

Everything in existence is vibrating energy.

We interpret this energy to be positive or negative, based on the vibrational frequency. Positive energy vibrates at a higher frequency than negative energy, and similar frequencies of energy unite together.

If we focus on emitting energy in a high frequency first, we in turn attract the same positive vibrations, thus amplifying and magnetizing an abundance of peace, love and happiness in our lives.

We can create positive vibrations by practicing affirmations of self-love and gratitude. Through the daily repetition of these rituals we clear old thought patterns, focus our time into the now, hence creating new pathways to form a peaceful and happy life.

By spending time connecting and worshipping our internal self, we are creating an open communication channel to our Soul, the Source of Creation, and shifting our state of consciousness closer to enlightenment.

To use this book, begin by creating your Sacred Altar and then when ready, refer to how to use this book to commence your Daily Rituals.

Preparation:
Create Your Sacred Alter

Your sacred altar is a personal place for you to harness spiritual energy. It is your own space of tranquil harmony, and therefore is a perfect area for worship, meditation and to recite rituals. Through the daily practice of honoring your altar, you will create a line of clear communication to realign with Source, your Higher Self, the Eternal Spirit within.

To begin, find an area in your house that you can call your own. It can be an area of any size, and any texture of surface.

Collect physical objects to represent the energetic elements of Earth, Air, Water, Fire and Spirit and place them around your altar in their own elemental area of your choice.

Personal decorations around your sacred space can be added as you please, for this is a shrine for you, so include anything that makes you happy. The below ideas are suggestions only as your perception of the elemental energy is your interpretation alone, and therefore you can use anything you would like to embody these energies.

Earth is connected to nature and provides grounding, security and harvesting. Symbols for Earth may be a crystal, plant, a bowl of dirt or salt.

Water represents our emotional wellbeing. It is used for reflection, healing and nurturing. Symbols for Water could be a jar of water, a shell or a small bowl.

Air signifies knowledge, courage, clarity and detachment. Suggested ideas for Air could be a feather, essential oil, incense or a bell.

Fire initiates creative and sexual energy, strength and protection. To represent Fire you could use a candle, wood, or something of the color red.

Spirit is our eternal self, the Source of Life Force Energy. To symbolize Spirit you could use a mirror, a crystal sphere, an image of yourself or ancestor, or a figurine of some kind.

As you commence your daily ritual, move around the altar as you please. Allow yourself the freedom to be drawn to the elements in whatever way you wish. Everyone is different and there is no right or wrong way to do it.

Through the repetition of holding space for yourself at your altar, you will identify a calm and peaceful state of emotional wellbeing immediately upon view. Any stress, worry or fear will quickly diminish as you continue to practice switching your mind frame to positivity, peace and harmony.

Keep a blank journal and pen next to your altar, for this will also become useful as you deepen your practice of Daily Rituals. As we express ourselves openly in our journal we can explore ourselves more intensely by documenting visions and thoughts, as well as identifying where it is that we are being held back from our own happiness. Through reflection we can see how the pain and emotion that once felt so real has now passed, and that the hurt has turned into admiration for the growth that has occurred as a direct result of the challenge we once faced. Observing ourself as we review these experiences, and setting our intentions, motivates and builds a strong mindset for everyone to accomplish great things.

This sacred space is your creation; a powerful potion to gather and manifest positive energies from. It is an area of protection and a place to cultivate inspiration.

How to Use your
Daily Rituals Book

To commence your Daily Ritual, open your space in a way that resonates with you. It could be through lighting a candle, ringing a bell, burning some incense, or tapping objects in a rhythmic order to acknowledge their presence. Upon doing so, close your eyes and imagine the elemental energy connecting with your energy field. There is an abundance of energy here for you, and it is ready for you to harness.

Take 3 deep breaths and open your book at random, or choose a word from the table of contents that you feel drawn to. This is your Daily Ritual. Recite the chosen Daily Ritual out loud to yourself.
Listen carefully as you hear the words and observe how you feel.

Read the definition of the affirmation and be dedicated in deepening your understanding. Take a moment to allow the words to sink in. Follow the daily exercise and journal work. Some exercises require outside influence, if it is not possible for that day, move on to the journal work and refer back to it later.

Any affirmations that you feel uneasy with requires extra attention. Write the affirmation down and place it around your house. Throughout the day continue to repeat the affirmation frequently, and again before sleeping that night. Take note of any improvement.

Daily Rituals

Positive Affirmations to attract Love,

Happiness and Peace.

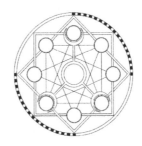

I Love Myself

Define: When you truly love and accept yourself just as you are, you will feel a complete sense of peace and harmony in your body and soul. You will glow with radiant beauty from the inside of your essence thus decorating your entire world in an abundance of love. You will respectfully portray the love that you wish to attract which is a vital key to creating long lasting relationships. When you love yourself whole heartedly, you will be overflowing with loving energy, infectiously passing this love on to everyone around you. From your positive nature and beautiful loving energy, you will be a joy to be around, and your life will be full of happiness and peace.

Exercise: Stand in front of the mirror and look at yourself directly in the eyes. Say to yourself - "I love you". Repeat this self-love affirmation 3 times with a deep breath in-between. Be sincere. Allow any thoughts to rise from it, whether negative or positive. Repeat this affirmation several times throughout the day and incorporate this affirmation into your life whenever you look into the mirror. Over time, you will become comfortable talking to yourself in this manner and the love for yourself will reflect in the life around you.

Journal: Deepen your understanding by writing down what unconditional love means to you. List the qualities and attributes in yourself that you love.

To help with this, finish the following sentences:

To me, unconditional love is . . .

I love myself because . . .

I love everyone around me because . . .

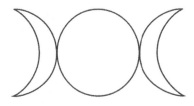

My Intuition is Loud and Clear and I Listen as it Shines Brightly

Define: As we dance through life we are constantly faced with challenges and excitement. The decision to steer away or thrive through these challenges are guided to us by our intuition (sometimes also referred to as 'gut instinct'). Our intuition is here to guide us on the right path. If we practice listening to our intuition regularly, the line of communication between ourself and our internal dialogue will become strong, and we will triumph over any situation. There will be no fear of making a wrong decision for we have faith and trust in our intuition.

Exercise: Regular meditation is a definite way to strengthen your connection to your intuition. By clearing your mind and connecting to Source, you are creating space for your intuition to ring through loud and clear. Meditate for 10-15 minutes daily. While meditating, envision a blue colored light that begins in your heart, shooting up through your throat, and out of the crown of your head. Send this light energy to the stars above, and completely open yourself up to receive the answers.

Journal: Think of a question you would like to ask your intuition. It can be one or many questions. Focus on the question and repeat it in your mind. When ready, write the question down in your journal, and without thinking or pausing, write an answer immediately. Daily practice of question and answers with your inner voice will help strengthen your connection.

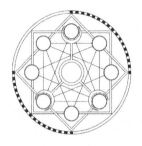

I Am Surrounded
With Love

Define: You are never alone. There is always an abundance of love surrounding you. This love can be found through your family and friends, or even in a perfect stranger on the street. But, the strongest, most affluent love to exist comes from Mother Nature. The Earth, the sun, the moon and the stars are all filled with loving energy; as is the ground upon which you walk, the air you breathe and the water you drink. There are beautiful animals, insects, birds, mammals, creatures of all kinds and flora and fauna all around you. Take the time to connect with Mother Nature and feel the love that she gifts to you.

Exercise: Today, acknowledge and give gratitude to the love that surrounds you. Think of 5 people who love you for you (alive or spirit, and yourself is included). Imagine them clearly, feel the loving connection between you and say "thank you" for their unconditional love. When you walk outside today, look at the Earth, the sun and moon around you, and give thanks to whatever crosses your path. Practice gratitude and in return, love will blossom.

Journal: After completing the above exercise, write down the people in your life who love you, and the gifts from Mother Nature that crossed your path.

Finish this sentence:

I am surrounded with love because . . .

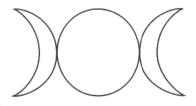

My Higher Self is Always Looking After Me

Define: Your Higher Self is the real You in pure enlightenment. It is the source of all energy, creation and consciousness. You are always connected to your Higher Self, as it is there watching over you, making sure you are receiving all the appropriate lessons and the experiences that you need. There is no need to be fearful of not receiving what it is that you truly desire, for your Higher Self will deliver it to you in the divine time.

Exercise: Close your eyes and take 5 deep breaths as you connect back to Source. Clear your mind into a meditative state of consciousness. Imagine a fire of light in your heart, and envision it to open up a pathway through your eyes, up to your third eye, and through the crown of your head. Here is the channel into your Higher Self. Talk to You.

Journal: Connection to your Higher Self will result in expanded knowledge, greater wisdom and in becoming more yourself. Through consistently listening to your Higher Self, you are able to confidently go about your day. Write down any subject that you wish to have help with from your Higher Self. It could be a manifestation to achieve a goal, or perhaps a desire to let something go. Write it down, take a deep breath, and release the thought. Allow your Higher Self to take care of it. Be open to the signs and listen.

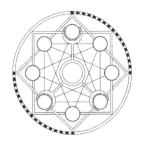

I Vibrate Light from My Soul and Create Harmony around Me

Define: The energy inside of you is pure and sacred. You emit energy and likewise absorb energy around you. What kind of energy do you wish to radiate and attract? Is there anything or anyone surrounding you that is depleting your own energy? As you start to take notice of energetic fields, you will natural navigate towards positive vibrations. Just as energy is emitted, and absorbed it can also be replenished. And mother nature supplies us with an abundance of resources to replenish our energy!

Exercise: Spending time in nature is the best way to re-energize yourself and purify your thoughts and energy. Go somewhere where you can immerse yourself in nature and stand still. Close your eyes and take 3 deep breaths. When you open your eyes, walk towards your first attraction. Allow the energy to pull you near. Look carefully — what do you see? Look at the detail of the gift from Mother Nature; this beauty is a pure energy vibration. It is here to cleanse and clear your mind, and remind you of how beautiful the world is. Give gratitude for this gift. Now look at your hands, can you see the same beauty in them? Keep looking at yourself until you do.

Journal: Write down what your home environment is like. Is it full of love? Are you at peace? Are you happy? Identify the areas that you wish to improve on, write them down. Next, write down the solutions on how you can implement these changes to make your home environment a pleasurable place. What about your work? Is it a pleasurable place to be in? Can you make some improvements to help this? Small crystals or a plant at your desk, or even focus on connecting with co-workers, customers to improve your life experience at work. Lastly, your relationships. Are there any relationships that are draining your energy as opposed to uplifting it? Choose the right relationships that are only compliment your positive loving energy.

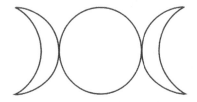

I Can Do Anything
I Set My Mind To

Define: You are the creator of your universe. Anything you wish to achieve in this life is available to you. You have the freedom of choice. You can choose to be happy. You can choose to pursue your dreams. You can choose to live a peaceful life. Making the decision is the first step, you also need to follow through with an action plan. To achieve your ultimate dreams and desires, you need to believe in yourself, and your goal, and believe that it is possible. Set your intention and follow through with action.

Exercise: What would you like to achieve today/this week/month/year/ life? Set your intention and speak as though it is already done. Give gratitude for the gift of today and stay positive that all will come true. The key to attaining your true abundance is through manifestation and aligning your energy to match the manifested frequency. To do this you must remove any negative thoughts or ideas that are holding you back. Open your mind to clearly envision the goals you wish to achieve. Imagine what achieving your objectives would feel like, taste like and be like? Envision this vibrational frequency regularly. Have faith in your pure intentions and allow the universe to work its magic.

Journal: Write down your dreams, aspirations and goals. Make the list as long as you would like! With each dream that you have chosen, write down the steps that it takes to achieve it. How will you do it? Create a clear pathway for you to follow through and attain your aspirations. If you have something similar like this in place already, check in and see how you measure against your time frames. Reward yourself for achieving your desired milestones, or if not, figure out how you can allocate more time to pursue your dreams.

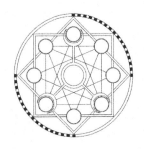

All the Answers
I Seek are Within Me

Define: You hold the answer to every question you could ever ask, all you need to do is close your eyes and listen. This is your world, your creation. Everything exists because you decide it to. You are creating every second of it. Have faith in yourself, and know that you are safe, because you have the answer within you. Through regular practice of meditation, and opening a clear pathway to communicate with your Higher Self, you can reveal the answer to any question that you wish.

Exercise: Repeat the daily affirmation 3 times with deep breaths in between. Ask for guidance from your Higher Self to communicate to you through your intuition. Next, ask yourself a question that can only be answered by 'yes' or 'no' (rephrase the question as necessary). As you recite the question again, say 'yes' and 'no' and feel the weight of each answer speak truth from your heart - whichever answer is lighter is the correct one. If no answer can be determined at this time, then it is not the right time to make the decision. Calmly wait for another day and repeat.

Journal: Write your chosen affirmation and believe the depth of this truth. Close your eyes and ask for guidance from your intuition. Think carefully about the question you desire to be answered. Speak it slowly in your mind, and out loud. Write the question down on the paper and immediately after, write the answer without thinking. Be open to accepting whatever is told to you.

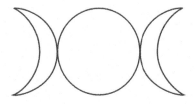

I Am Stronger than I was Yesterday

Define: Experience is what makes us stronger. The challenges, the heartache, the grief, the happiness and the pleasure. Every experience, whether it is good or bad, provides us with the tools for the future. Every step of the way is building up our courage and confidence to take greater risks in the direction of what it is that we truly want and love. It is accessible to everyone. We just need to believe in your own strength and ability.

Exercise: Do some yoga stretches to give love back to your body. Stand tall with your feet flat on the floor, hip width apart. Reach up high to the stars. Feel the stretch between your bones and take 3 deep breaths. Feel the air circulating through your veins as it provides energy in your body. Slowly bend down to touch your toes and kiss your knees. Hold here for 3 breaths. Repeat 3 times. You are alive. Give thanks for the strength that you carry.

Journal: Gratitude in turn attracts more gratitude. Write down 3 experiences that have shaped you for the better, that were once a struggle but ultimately worked out for the best and that you learned from. Applaud yourself for your courage and determination. Remind yourself to be flexible in your approach to life. Even though situations will continue to challenge us, we can control our reactions, and it is here that our greatest strength lies.

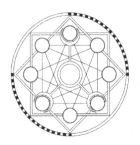

I Am True to Myself and I have Strong Boundaries in Place

Define: You have the freedom to choose your attitude, beliefs and morals in your life. And from these beliefs of what is important to you, you then create boundaries for acceptable behavior around you. Once boundaries are established, it is your responsibility to adhere that these boundaries are communicated clearly. Likewise, it is your responsibility to ensure that you are acting ethically in accordance to what you perceive to be right and wrong.

Exercise: Remove anything or anyone who disturbs your peaceful way of life. Take 3 deep breath to calm yourself and close your eyes. Ask yourself - "Is there is anyone or anything that I need to remove from my life that is not in alignment to my ultimate well-being?" Take note of whatever comes up, be it a memory, a vision, a thought, or an idea. Focus on '*this*', thank it for the lesson, and create a new boundary that will benefit your well-being. Follow through implementing this boundary for the current situation and make note to refer back to this if ever a similar situation arises again. In your daily life, make a conscious effort to avoid any negativity by removing yourself from the situation.

Journal: Write down your beliefs and boundaries of what is acceptable and unacceptable behavior to you. Reflect on yourself to determine whether you are acting in accordance with this list. Are there any people or situations that do not honor your boundaries? If so, disconnect yourself from harmful situations to protect your energy. This is an act of self-love and self-respect. Refer back to your list often and update it as necessary.

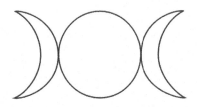

Today, Everything that has been Manifested will come into Fruition

Define: You are the creator of your universe and everything that you imagine has the possibility of coming true. There are no limits. The only limits to exist are the limits you place on yourself. Everything is attainable and everything is within your reach. You need to set your intention, and then vibrate your energy at the equally matched frequency. Once this is achieved, the manifestation will come into form.

Exercise: Think about what it is that you want manifested on this day. Imagine the idea to be real. See it, feel it, taste it, hear it, smell it. Allow yourself to be completely immersed in this manifestation. Feel the way your body would feel if it were to come true. Light the flame of a candle, or imagine a fire in your mind. Stare intently at the flame and repeat the manifestation loudly 3 times, taking deep breaths in between. Close your eyes and repeat today's affirmation. Acknowledge your blessings around your sacred altar and give gratitude. Extinguish the flame and take another deep breath.

Journal: Write down what it is that you wish to manifest. If it is an aspiration, write down goals to take the steps towards it. If it is a miraculous desire, clear your mind and allow peace and light to travel towards the existence. Repeat daily until the next full moon. When the full moon comes, use the 'Full Moon Ritual' at the end of this book.

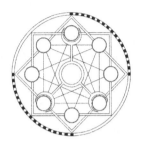

My Soul Dances in the Mystical Realm of Enchantment

Define: The world is a beautiful and joyous place if we dare to open our eyes and perceive it this way. Look around you . . . There is so much love, laughter and happiness surrounding you always! It is there, just waiting for you to acknowledge and appreciate it. The more light and love that you give gratitude to, the more that will come your way.

Exercise: Today, plan or do something that makes your heart sing! Go dancing, share a meal with a loved one, climb a mountain or go for a bush walk . . . do something that you have been wanting to do but keep putting off! The time is now! Take back control of the happiness in your life.

Journal: Write down activities that make you happy. This list can be as long as you wish. These things could be by yourself, in groups, or even ideas that you are yet to try out but you think you might like! Make an effort to fulfill these dreams and desires throughout the year ahead. Set yourself time frames upon which you wish to achieve these and review and renew this list often.

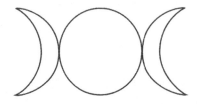

I Feel Angels around Me

Define: Energy is both indestructible and infinite. Therefore, our loved ones who have passed over to the other side never leave us. We are constantly surrounded by their loving energy and they visit us often to check up on us. We are also visited by angels from past lives and curious spirits. They radiate peace and loving energy always.

Exercise: Think of a loved one who has passed over and call out to them by name. Or perhaps if you have a curious spirit that you feel nearby, acknowledge them by the name, 'Angel'. Say whatever your heart desires. Give gratitude for their care and admiration. Wish a blessing for them and for you. Tell them that you are listening, should they wish to communicate.

I.e. - "Angel, thank you so much for your continuous love and support. Please send me signs for I am always listening."

Journal: If you wish to ask for a guided blessings from our angels, or perhaps are curious to know more, write to them through your journal. When writing to them, ask a question and immediately write down the answer. The angels will communicate to you through your inner voice, and the knowledge that is passed on is 'known' to you, without needing justification. Allow miracles to manifest from the love of angels around you.

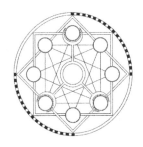

I Nourish My Body with Love and Respect

Define: At every moment our thoughts and actions are either beneficial or detrimental to our wellbeing. Choose to shower your body with love and affection and watch how it thrives! By accepting your body exactly as it is, you will love yourself more and in turn feel incredible! Pamper your body with the healthiest food, regular exercises and luscious indulgences such as baths, creams and self-massages.

Exercise: Treat yourself! Relax in a luxurious bath with some bath salts or a few drops of calming essentials oils such as rosemary or lavender. Soak and unwind. If you do not have access to a bath, have a beautiful warm shower and feel the droplets of water wash over your skin. Imagine the water to clear out anything unnecessary. Once clean, pamper your skin with luscious cream. Start at your feet and lather your way up to the tip of your head. Slowly massage yourself along the way and give thanks to each bone and muscle for its strength in your body.

Journal: Write down the way you feel about your body. Be completely open and honest. State what you love and if there is anything you do not love, write it down too. Go over the notes you have written and anywhere you have spoken negatively about your body, change the words to be encouraging and positive. By continuously speaking positive thoughts about your body you will want to look after yourself the way you deserve.

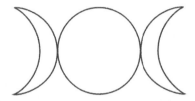

I Forgive and Let Go

Define: Holding onto pain or anger only hurts yourself. It does not hurt anyone around you, only yourself. When you forgive and let go of this trouble on your heart, space will be opened up to allow new experiences to come forth to you. Pain and anger are detrimental thoughts, it is negative energy that you are holding onto. It's time to let it go. It's only a thought, and it's not providing you any joy, happiness or peace. Let it go.

Exercise: Is there someone in your life who you need to forgive? Remember that this could be yourself. Envision the person/yourself who you need to forgive. Repeat the following words: "I forgive you. I love you. Thank you for the lesson. I release you." Repeat this 3 times, speaking to the person you envision. Imagine a gold cord between you two, and cut the cord. This will release the old 'hurt' and allow a new energy vibration to filter through to you.

Journal: Write down any problems in your life — any people or situations that you need to let go of. Write a pretend letter to them, saying that you forgive them, that you appreciate the lesson, that you love them and that you release them. After going through each name and situation, acknowledge the openness that you now feel in your heart. Sit with this, pausing for several breaths as you allow new energy to form.

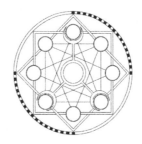

I Believe in Myself

Define: You are the only one who needs to believe in yourself to accomplish anything in this life. You were born alone and you will die alone. What you do between this time of birth and death is entirely up to you, it relies on no one else. You can succeed at anything you want and you can live the life that you have always dreamed of. All you need to do is believe in yourself.

Exercise: Look in the mirror. Take a deep breath and repeat - "I believe in you. You can do this." Repeat this affirmation 3 times, taking a deep breath in between each. Say this affirmation as much as you like. By speaking positive and supportive words to yourself, you are creating strength in your mind, body and soul. This strength of happiness and positivity will be reflected on those around you.

Journal: Mark the top of the page with the affirmation "I believe in Myself". Underneath write down 5 reasons as to why you believe in yourself. Talk about your strengths and your ability to create anything you put your mind to. Write down any goals or aspirations that require beliefs in yourself. Set the intention and write the steps down you need to take to achieve your dreams.

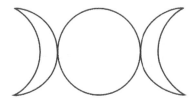

My Spirit Guides are with Me at All Times

Define: There is nothing to worry about because your Spirit Guides are looking after you. They are always with you, and loyally guiding you on this journey. All the lessons you wish to learn were planned out between your Spirit Guides and your Higher Self long before you entered this Earth, and therefore your experiences in this life are always being looked after.

Exercise: Talk to your Spirit Guides. Imagine what your Spirit Guide/s might look like. Envision them. Talk to them. Make a name for them. Be grateful for their time and ask them what it is that you need to know today. Be open to receive and listen to the answer with an open heart. Look for the signs around you. Your Spirit Guides are talking to you everyday.

Journal: Using the same exercise above, draw your Spirit Guides. It can be anything — from a shape, to a butterfly, to a stick figure. Additionally, write down their name or a name that you feel comfortable with. Remember, that because everything is energy, you are creating a symbol to communicate with that energy so there is no right or wrong answer. Be open-minded and allow the Spirit to talk through to you. Engage with your Spirit Guides regularly and ask them any questions you wish to know.

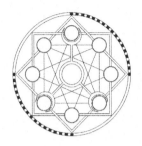

I Let Go of My Fears and Trust that All Is Okay

Define: There is nothing to be feared in this world. Fear is only the repercussion of misunderstanding. Whenever you feel the thoughts of fear creep into your subconscious, ask yourself why it is there. What is it here to teach you? Face the fear, feel the emotion, accept the lesson, then let go and move on. Try to look at your fear with the mind frame of giving it love. Perhaps the fear resolves around a problem that lacks information? By changing the way we perceive our fears, we are able to recreate our experience and expectation.

Exercise: Ask yourself "What is it that I fear today?" Listen carefully to the answer. Ask yourself how you can better understand the root of the fear? Where does the insecurity lie? What lack of understanding does it need to know. And can love solve this problem? Hold the fear tightly and tell it - "I love myself, I trust that my Higher Self is guiding me, and that this fear cannot hurt me. All will be okay." Then release this thought, never to enter your mind again.

Journal: As per the above exercise, ask yourself what it is that you fear and write it down. Address the issue directly at hand by writing yourself a letter. Tell yourself why this fear is irrelevant, and turn it around into an optimistic viewpoint. By reviewing the issues in a positive light, you will identify the old fear in this new thought pattern, and the fear will quickly diminish thereafter.

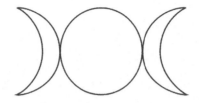

I Let Go of Regret and Create Space for New Beginnings

Define: Everything in your life has led you to where you are today. You are stronger, wiser and better than you were yesterday because of it. Never regret anything, because it was your choice and you need to stand by your choice. Even if you feel as though it was a mistake, that mistake has now steered your life into a different direction, and in time when you look back, it will all make sense. You need to trust the process. There is no point in worrying about the past, it is wasted energy. When we let go of pain, anger or regret, we open up the space for something better to be created.

Exercise: Ask yourself, what is your biggest regret? Close your eyes and imagine the centre of your heart. Envision it as a glowing fire inside of you. Throw your regret into the fire of your heart and allow it to be burned up. Repeat the words "I let go of all regret and allow the space to be opened up for new beginnings." Repeat 3 times.

Journal: Write down what it is that you regret and the reason why. Review the regret and turn it into something positive. This can be done by writing the lessons that you learned from your past mistakes. Write to yourself saying how proud you are for having self-awareness for what has happened. For you now have learned to not make the same mistake twice. And reflection that leads to self-awareness is one of the wisest and most important attributes of someone's personality.

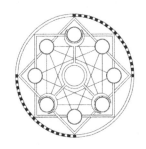

I Am Kind, Nurturing and Loving to Myself

Define: Looking after your health is vital to your well-being. Health includes your body, mind and soul as a whole. Be mindful of your thoughts, your words and your actions. Ensure that you are eating healthy food and participating in light exercise on a regular basis. Most importantly, take time to connect back to your heart and your Higher Self daily. By adapting these simple changes to your lifestyle you will have more energy, feel more at peace and be happier with yourself. Through giving love to yourself, you in turn give love to the rest of the world.

Exercise: Today - be kind to your body. Start the day with a few yoga stretches. Intuitively move the way your body feels like it needs to stretch. Take a few deep breaths. Go for a casual walk around your neighborhood. Notice 3 things that are beautiful that you hadn't seen before. Nourish your body with only healthy and nutritious food. No sugar, meat, or dairy. Eat plentiful greens, vegetables and fruit. Meditate for 15 minutes. Set your intentions for the day and repeat the affirmation, "I am kind, nurturing and loving to myself."

Journal: What do you eat? How much exercise do you do? Document your activities for a week and have a good look at what you are doing. Are you exercising at least 3 times a week? Are you eating enough plant based foods? Are you drinking enough water? Have a look at where you can improve your health. It can start as baby steps, but aim to make one small change a day, and increase as time permits.

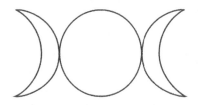

I have Unlimited Energy Flowing within Me that I Can Access at Any Time

Define: We have an unlimited amount of energy vibrating inside of us continuously. It is 'we' who directs the energy and decides for it to be active or dormant. It is we who uses this energy to our advantage or disadvantage. Your energy is in abundance and never ending, ready to be utilized however you so desire. There is no end to this energy. The more energy we use the more energy we create.

Exercise: Stand tall. Shake your body from feet, through your hands to your head. Wiggle quickly and fluidly. Feel your blood moving through your body. Now close your eyes and take 5 very deep breaths. Inhale slowly and exhale slowly. One after the other. You can be sitting or standing. Open your eyes and feel the loving energy pulsating through your veins!

Journal: How do you wish to use this energy? Is there a project that you have been putting off? Perhaps something creative that you enjoy doing that you don't do anymore? Creative energy comes in all forms, it can be manual (using your hands), imaginative, or physical. Write down at least 3 of your favorite things that you enjoy using your energy for. They could be cooking, playing a musical instrument, painting or gardening. Make sure you incorporate these activities into your lifestyle on a weekly basis.

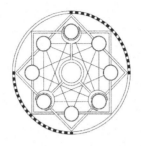

I Am Blessed

Define: YES YOU ARE! You are a divine creation of the universe. You radiate beauty, love and joy. You hold a gift for the world, and your purpose in life is to share your gift with everyone. By being true to yourself and staying connected to your Higher Self, you will forever be blessed. You are always surrounded with love and peace. You just need to open your eyes and see it, close your eyes and feel it, and open your heart to receive it.

Exercise: Today, give gratitude to everything and everyone who comes your way. Say thank you for the food you receive and water you drink. As you interact with people today, be thankful for their time and presence and compliment them graciously. By incorporating gratitude, you will see how beautifully blessed your life is and more blessings will magnetically flow towards you.

Journal: List all the amazing blessings in your life! Add as many things as you can think of, small or big! Everything counts, and as you look over this beautiful list of blessings, give gratitude and realize how blessed you truly are. Keep adding to this list as much as you can and review it often, remembering the beautiful warm feeling of having such blessings in your life.

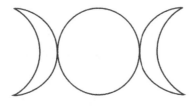

My Happiness is a Choice that I Make Every Day

Define: The decision to be happy is a choice that we consciously choose every day. There will always be reasons to be sad, but there are also many more reasons to be happy. Negative thoughts are here to teach us a lesson, and as you begin to identify the lack of self-love behind the negative thought, will you be able to grow through it. When a negative thought comes into your mind, challenge it! Tell it the reasons why it is incorrect, show it why positivity will triumph over it. You have the power to choose which side you wish to listen to. And the more effort you make into seeing the positives in life, the more natural the decision to be happy will become. As you grow stronger in your connection to Spirit and intuition, it will become easier to acknowledge and dismiss the bad to be able to focus on the good.

Exercise: Look in the mirror and say to yourself, "Today, I choose happiness." Repeat 3 times between 3 deep breaths. Listen to the words and truly comprehend what they mean. Acknowledge this thought and then release it, letting go any negative connotations that may have surfaced. Whenever negative thoughts arrive say, "Thank you, I am listening and I release you. I choose happiness today."

Journal: Finish this sentence: "I am happy because . . ." Write down as many things as you feel happy about. Make an effort to visit or do these things everyday. Next address any negative thoughts that continue to haunt you. Write through it to understand why you are feeling this way. And then, turn the thought around to be positive. Play with other possibilities as to why the positive would be true. And ask yourself - if you loved yourself and believed that you were truly looked after by your Higher Self, would this negative thought exist?

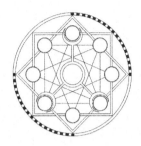

Every Choice I Make Belongs to Me and No One Else

Define: You are powerful beyond measure. It is both your right and your freedom to make your own choices to decide upon what is best for yourself and your future. It is no one else's power but your own, and no one else will know the answer better than yourself. You have the knowledge and the wisdom to make the right decisions for you, you just need to believe in yourself.

Exercise: Look into the mirror and take a deep breath. Repeat out loud: "I am powerful and incredible. I know what is best for me and I stand by the decisions I make." Be strong in your choices! If you find that you have difficulty choosing an answer, simply be at peace knowing that it is not the right time to make that decision, and when the time comes you will know the answer.

Journal: Do you feel uneasy about a choice you have to make? Write down the decision that needs to be made, and then write down the best possible outcome. Then write down the worst possible outcome. Then write down an outcome that would make you happy. Open your heart and seek guidance to choose. Again, if you cannot choose, it is not the right time to make that decision.

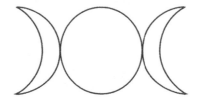

I Am At Peace

Define: Peace is here and ready for you, if only you were willing to accept it! Being at peace is something that only you can choose to feel. Peace is attained through dissolving thoughts of all kinds, and surrendering yourself completely into the moment. Do not worry about the past, or be anxious for the future. Enjoy everything that is happening in the very now of your being. Get outside of your head and feel yourself in your body. Feel the lightness of your being, admire your beautiful surroundings and embrace limitless love in all its glory.

Exercise: Ask yourself, what is it that brings you peace? And, how often do you gift yourself this peace? Make a conscious effort to incorporate this act of peace every day. Some ideas could be listening to music, lighting a candle, drawing, painting, sitting in nature, going for a walk. And of course, meditation is the easiest way to calm your mind. Whatever it is that provides you clarity and calmness, do it.

Journal: Write down the things that brings you peace. List 5 things. Write down why they provide you this peace. Write down how often you do each of these things. Can you improve this? Write down the reasons why you are not at peace. How can you change this? By identifying where you are not at peace in contrast to where you are, you will be able to attain clarity and harmony through your actions and decisions. The decision to be at peace will grace your presence without you needing to search for it.

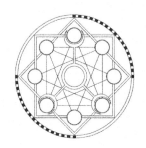

Every Relationship is Complimentary to My World

Define: You are unique, beautiful and powerful. You have the freedom to choose who you surround yourself with. Choose your friends and lovers wisely. They should bring only positive light to you and compliment, support and encourage your way of life. Your relationship with yourself is the most important relationship that you can have. Be completely devoted to you by submerging yourself with love, and respect and ensure that anyone who comes into your circle is worthy of your time.

Exercise: If you are surrounded with positive people, and you are happy with the relationships around you, acknowledge and appreciate them. Any relationships (both friendship or love) that you feel heavy from, is attracting negative energy into your life. It might be time to end these, or energetically disconnect from them. To do so, close your eyes and imagine this person. Envision a gold cord between the two of you, and cut it. Be grateful for the lesson, and tell the person loudly "I release you." The energy between you two is now cut. Make an effort to physically detach yourself in daily life too.

Journal: Describe the relationship with yourself. Do you love and accept yourself unconditionally? Do you take care of yourself? Nurture your body and mind with love and respect? By creating a healthy relationship with ourselves, we set the standard of the relationship we expect from others. For it is through our love for self that we teach others what we deserve and expect.

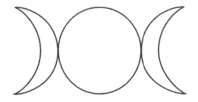

I Am in Harmony
with My Body

Define: How often do you listen to your body? Truly and honestly listen to it? By nourishing you body with healthy food you heal yourself and build strength in your mind. A well-planned plant based diet has and still is the most beneficial and ethical food regime since the beginning of time. Through eating only fruit and vegetables you provide your cells with all the fuel they need to fight any illness because your organs and muscles will perform at the ultimate level. By following a vegan diet you are not destroying the environment, nor absorbing negative energies from terrified and slaughtered animals. When you are in tune with your body you will know immediately if you digest something that is not complementary to your wellbeing.

Exercise: Have a look in your cupboard at home. How much of your food is nutritious and beneficial to your body? Anything that is not serving your highest good, donate or throw it out. Make an effort today to only eat healthy food that nourishes and nurtures your body. Ultimate health is through a vegan, dairy-free, meat-free, sugar-free, gluten-free diet. Sounds complex? It's actually quite easy when you update your kitchen! Your body and mind will thank you for it, and the decision to eat healthier becomes easier and easier each day.

Journal: List the things that make your body happy. Examples of these things are yoga, walking, eating certain foods, having green smoothies. Take note of the things that you notice a difference with when you incorporate them into your daily lifestyle. Be sure to do more of these things, or if you already do them, find likeminded projects you can continue to challenge yourself with. Never stop learning.

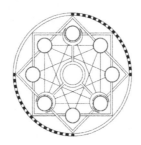

I Am a Positive Light who Inspires Others

Define: You are brilliant, beautiful and a positive person to be around. Every person in your life is influenced by you in some way. Especially children, who are extra impressionable as they are constantly seeking to understand themselves and do so by their outside peers. Adults admire you too, so pay close attention to your attitude. By exuding a positive belief system in place, you will encourage others to do the same and in return generate a happy and peaceful environment around you.

Exercise: Observe the way you act today as you interact with other people. Do you speak truth? Do you talk with honesty and integrity about yourself and others? Do you promote a beautiful and optimistic outlook on your life and compliment others on theirs? Anytime you notice yourself swaying to the negative side, pick yourself up and change direction. Be the reason someone smiles today.

Journal: Write down the reasons why you are a strong role model for others. List your qualities that are inspiring and positive. Do you speak with integrity? Are you honest, a good listener? Acknowledge and review the beauty in your character. It's also good to list things that you would like to improve on as well. By being truthful with yourself, and addressing your weaknesses, you are able to change these into positives.

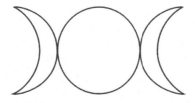

I Can Heal Myself

Define: We are the creators of our world, and therefore we create negative or positive influences that affect it. Sickness in the body or mind is a cry for help, and a desperate need for change. Are you taking care of yourself? Are you feeding your body with a plant-based nutrients and light exercise daily? Do you love yourself? Are you taking time by yourself to meditate and recharge? A physical illness is the result of an internal and emotional problem. If we concentrate on healing our mind and thoughts, we will heal ourselves and educate others to heal the world around us.

Exercise: Physical pain is the result of an emotional blockage, or unhealthy diet. These are the two main causes for illness and disease. It is so important to ensure that you have healed yourself, your mind and your past to be able to move forward. If you are dealing with a sickness, figure out how and why this sickness occurred, look to metaphysical realms and research understanding. What is it that you are fearful of? Have you released your emotional pain from the past? Seek natural medicines and alternative therapies, follow a plant-based diet and meditate often. It is important to educate yourself both emotionally and physically as to why the illness has occurred in order for you to heal yourself.

Journal: Write down where you are feeling pain. Then, try and remember any other times that you have felt this pain before. Refer to family members, have they experienced a similar pain that you are going through? Envision the pain and answer the questions. What color is the pain? What size is the pain? If you were to identify the pain with an emotion what would it be? Try to recall an incident that occurred when you felt that emotion. Write it down. Acknowledge and accept the pain from that emotion. Release and let go. It's time to move on.

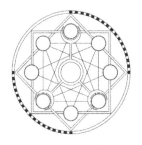

I Am Healthy
and Beautiful

Define: The most powerful words you can say are - 'I am'. It is so important to use them carefully and to always promote a positive and loving description of yourself. How often do you give yourself a compliment, speak about your beautiful face and body, or your intelligent mind and loving heart? The more we say it, the more we believe it, and the easier it will be for others to see the truth too.

Exercise: Stand straight in front of a mirror. Look at yourself, your face and body. Repeat the affirmation 3 times in between 3 deep breaths and relax. Look at yourself carefully with no judgement, no thoughts, no anything. Just reflect. Try and look at yourself in the same positive light the same way that you would a friend. Focus on the positives of your face and body only. Lastly, smile to yourself.

Journal: Take a journal and write down at least 5 wonderful and positive qualities about yourself. Then repeat these out loud in the mirror. You can make the list as long as you like! And repeat this as often as you like! Say it until you believe it!

E.g - I am beautiful. I am healthy. I am a joy to be around. I am peaceful. I am love.

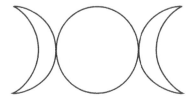

I Create My Reality

Define: This is one of the most empowering statements that you can make. It embodies the fact that you create EVERYTHING around you. And your attitude to life relies on how you perceive the events that surround you. You create your happiness, your sadness, your joy and your grief. Everything that is evolving around you is your miraculous creation. You choose to do with it what you wish. You have unlimited potential swimming around inside of you. Today it is time to feel the excitement and liberation of being able to control your own destiny!

Exercise: Take note of how beautiful the world is. Are you at peace in your mind? Are you doing what you love? Are you living where you love? Are you surrounded by people and places that you love? If the answer is no, ask yourself what you want to change. Figure out the steps to achieve this change and focus on it. Be realistic in terms of time frame and meditate every day for 15 minutes.

Journal: If you have recognized that there is something in your life that makes you unhappy, write down what an ideal scenario would be to change this. Next, write down the steps that you can take to achieve this. After that, write down a realistic time frame and measure the steps in reference to the time frame. Stick to it! You cannot complain about change if you do not do anything about it. And you are the creator, you have the power to create the life that you want - take control and have fun with it!

Personal Notes

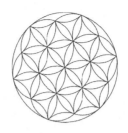

Self-Love Reminders

Tell Me all the Things You
Love about Yourself?

I love.. my strength, my wisdom and my courage.

My compassion, my kindness and my sensitivity.

My humor, my good heart and my positivity.

I love my loyalty, my creativity and intelligence.

My motivation, perseverance and passion.

My ability to love unconditionally, my honesty, and integrity.

My connection to self, to Source and to my intuition.

I love my independence, thoughtfulness, and uniqueness.

My open mind, my joy of making others laugh,

and my acceptance of change.

My self-discipline, my gratitude and my ability to dream big.

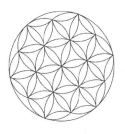

Commitment to Self

I focus all of my energy and attention into loving myself.

From the moment I wake up to the moment I fall asleep-

I am kind, nurturing and loving to myself.

I eat healthy food and listen to my body.

I spend time with people I care about, people who bring out the best in

me and people who share an equal exchange of energy.

I spend time by myself doing the things that I love.

I don't worry about anything,

because I know I am right

where I need to be.

And I know that everything is always working out

for my greatest good because I trust the divine timing of my life.

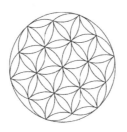

I AM

I am wonderful, beautiful, talented, and strong.

I am worthy, I am deserving, I am open to change.

I am magnificent beyond comprehension.

I am a divine soul who can accomplish anything I set my mind to.

I am in control of my thoughts, my mind and my body.

I accept responsibility for my actions.

I have all the answers I need right now.

I am more than enough.

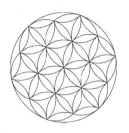

Energy Protection
Meditation

Close your eyes.

Take 3 deep breaths in and out.

Imagine a white light from above streaming down upon you
like a waterfall.

This light is pure, loving energy.

The light flows around you completely, and circles you
like a giant bubble.

This bubble of light is your sacred space.

You are safe here.

Nothing can harm you, nor come into your energy field.

Envision this bubble and say out loud:

"I command my sacred space."

This light is here to protect your energy.

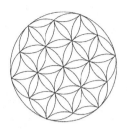

Full Moon Ritual

I invite the energy of the full moon into my essence.

And with gratitude and admiration, I inhale these gifts graciously.

Thank you for the light that blesses my body, my mind and my soul.

I welcome the light into my heart,

as it strengthens the connection between me and my Higher Self.

I feel the abundance of love surrounding me.

My manifestations are ripe and ready to burst with loving energy.

Please bless these creations and nurture them into fruition.

I wish for strength within myself.

To be true to myself and stand fully present in my own being.

Please provide me with the patience to accept what is,

and let go of everything that no longer serves me.

I wish for peace, happiness and health to everyone around me.

To my Angels and Spirit Guides, thank you for your loving support.

I love you. Thank you.

My moon, my love.

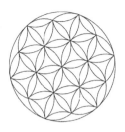

New Moon Journalling Questions

1. What is your new goal that you wish to achieve?

2. What new routine do you wish to embody?

3. What new qualities do you wish to attain?

4. What kind of life do you want to lead?

5. What are you grateful for?

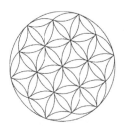

Morning Rituals

Cleanse + Refresh - Drink Water & take a Shower or Bath

Attract Abundance - Write down 3 things You are Grateful for

Connect with Mindfulness - Inhale + Exhale Five Deep Breaths

Ignite Clarity + Creativity - Burn Candles, Incense or Oils

Self-Heal - Meditate for 10-30 minutes

Be Open to Change - Stretch Your Body with Yoga or Dance

Manifestation - Write down Your Goals / Intentions for the Day

Nurture with Self-Love - Go for a Walk in Nature

Meet the Author

Phoebe Garnsworthy is an Australian female author who loves to discover magic in everyday life. She has traveled the world extensively, exploring eastern and western philosophies alike, while studying the influences that these beliefs have on humanity.

The intention of her writing is to encourage conscious living and unconditional love.

www.phoebegarnsworthy.com

www.lostnowhere.com